# CANADIAN BRASS
## SERIES OF COLLECTED QUINTETS

# IMMORTAL FOLKSONGS

**arranged for brass quintet**
**by Terry Vosbein**

## contents

2  Simple    Gifts

6  Shenandoah

1 0  Londonderry    Air

1 4  High    Barbary

2 1  Greensleeves

2 6  The    Drunken    Sailor

Welcome to the new *Canadian Brass Series of Collected Quintets*. In our work with students we have for some time been aware of the need for more brass quintet music at easy and intermediate levels of difficulty. We are continually observing a kind of "Renaissance" in brass music, not only in audience responses to our quintet, but to all brass music in general. The brass quintet, as a chamber ensemble, seems to have become as standard a chamber combination as a string quartet. That could not have been said twenty-five years ago. Brass quintets are popping up everywhere — professional quintets, junior and senior high school ensembles, college and university groups, and amateur quintets of adult players.

We have carefully chosen the literature for these collected quintets, and closely supervised the arrangements. Our aim was to retain a Canadian Brass flavor to each arrangement, and create attractive repertory designed so that any brass quintet can play it with satisfying results. We've often remarked to one another that we certainly wish that we'd had quintet arrangements like these when we were students!

Happy playing to you and your quintet.

— THE CANADIAN BRASS

## HAL•LEONARD®
### CORPORATION
7777 W. BLUEMOUND RD. P.O. BOX 13819 MILWAUKEE, WI 53213

# SIMPLE GIFTS

Traditional
*arranged by Terry Vosbein*

4

# SHENANDOAH

Traditional
*arranged by Terry Vosbein*

# Londonderry Air

Traditional
*arranged by Terry Vosbein*

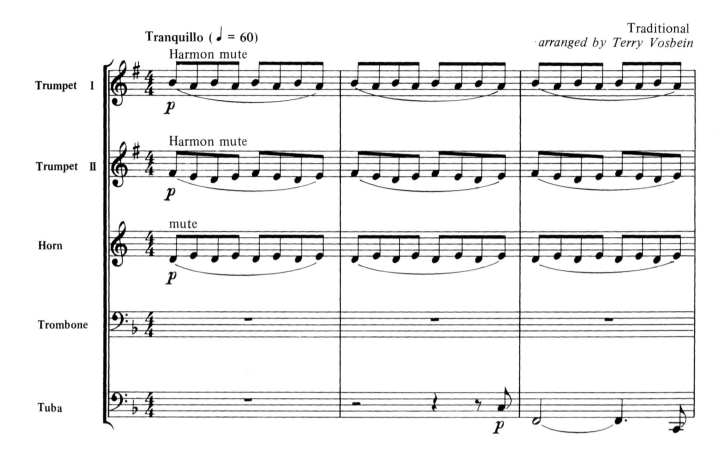

# HIGH BARBARY

Traditional
*Arranged by Terry Vosbein*

# GREENSLEEVES

Traditional
*arranged by Terry Vosbein*

# THE DRUNKEN SAILOR

Traditional
*arranged by Terry Vosbein*